THE HANDLESS MAIDEN

Jeremy Dobrish

BROADWAY PLAY PUBLISHING INC
New York
www.broadwayplaypublishing.com
info@broadwayplaypublishing.com

THE HANDLESS MAIDEN
© Copyright 1999 by Jeremy Dobrish

The play was first published in June 1999 in the collection *Plays By Jeremy Dobrish*

First printing, this edition, December 2010
I S B N: 978-0-88145-482-6

Book design: Marie Donovan
Page make-up: Adobe Indesign
Typeface: Palatino
Printed and bound in the U S A

ABOUT THE AUTHOR

Jeremy's plays include NOTIONS IN MOTION, BLINK OF AN EYE, SUPERPOWERS, and ORPHEUS AND EURYDICE all of which were produced by adobe theater company, and EIGHT DAYS (BACKWARDS) which was produced by the Vineyard Theater. All are published by Broadway Play Publishing Inc.

As a director, Jeremy has diretced in N Y C at Amas, M C C, Second Stage, N Y M F, N Y C Fringe, S P F, The Variety Arts Theater, The Century Center, The Promenade, W P A, The Kirk, SoHo Playhouse, Actor's Playhouse, The Zipper, Young Playwrights, etc.

Regionally he has directed at The Old Globe, Barrington Stage, North Shore, The O'Neill, New York Stage and Film, Goodspeed, and The Village Theater (Washington).

His adaptation of CURIOUS GEORGE and his productions of PAUL REVERE and VIRTUALLY ME tour the country with Theaterworks U S A.

Jeremy is the Co-Artistic of Midtown Direct Rep, has served as an Artistic Associate at Second Stage and was the Artistic Director of adobe theater company from 1991-2004. He is a member of the Dramatists Guild and S D C. www.jeremydobrish.com

THE HANDLESS MAIDEN was first presented by the adobe theatre company, opening on 25 February 1998. The cast and creative contributors were:

ERIC/MERLE	Vin Knight
ANN/CRONEY	Lia Yang
MAIDEN/JULIE/LISA	Molly Renfroe
DAVE/GARDENER/BARTENDER	Matthew Aibel
MILLER'S WIFE/MESSENGER	Janice O'Rourke
MILLER/MOE	Arthur Aulisi
DEVIL/MAX	Christopher Marobella
KING/PETER	Bryan Webster
Director	Damon Kiely
Sets	Steven Capone
Lighting	Christien Methot
Costumes	Carol Bailey
Sound	Chris Todd
Original music	Michael Garin

CHARACTERS

Note: The actors play more than one character. While it should be clear that it is the same actor, something should be done to make sure there is no confusion that it might be the same character, i.e., distinct costumes.

ERIC/MERLE
ANN/CRONE
MAIDEN/JULIE/LISA
DAVE/GARDENER/BARTENDER
MILLER'S WIFE/MESSENGER
MILLER/MOE
DEVIL/MAX
KING/PETER

MUSIC

When the adobe theatre company first presented the play in February 1998, we added some musical numbers that were written and arranged by Michael Garin. While they add a nice element of theatricality and I highly recommend using them, the play can be done without music. This script presents Michael's lyrics intact as well as ways to play the scenes without the songs. Should any producer desire to present the play with the music, they should contact Michael Garin for permission through Mitch Douglas at I C M, 212-556-5600. If the music is not used, the "Once upon a time's" at the top of scenes one, two, and three should be spoken rather than sung as indicated.

ACT ONE

(Prologue: Lights on ERIC *and* ANN *on opposite sides of the stage, driving. They each have a faraway look in their eyes. Lights up on the* MAIDEN. ANN *sings:)*

ANN: Once upon a time, a few weeks ago, in a faraway kingdom called New York City...

Scene One

*(*ANN *and* DAVE's. *Dinner. An open bottle of wine)*

ANN: O K, what about "Max"?

DAVE: No, God, I hate the name Max. I had an uncle Max who used to, you know the type, used to throw me in the pool when I was a little kid and scream, "It's the only way to learn how to swim, kick, you little twerp, kick for your life."

ANN: God, you have a problem with every single name.

DAVE: Well, what is with this name game all of a sudden? You're not pregnant?

ANN: Don't you think we should have a name in mind?

DAVE: Sure. But why now? Answer my question.

ANN: No, I'm not pregnant.

DAVE: So, then? Hey, you were the one, if I recall correctly, who said she wanted to be made partner first....

ANN: Yes...

DAVE: ...wanted more stability in our lives.

ANN: ...you recall correctly, counselor, that is what I said, but...

DAVE: Well, alright then. We stay on the plan. One of us gets made partner. Probably me. Then we start thinking family.

ANN: Well..., I have some interesting news.

DAVE: Yes?

ANN: Jacobson called me into his office today.

DAVE: Uh-huh?

ANN: They want to make me partner.

DAVE: Are you serious?

ANN: That's what he said.

DAVE: Why didn't you tell me?

ANN: I did just tell you.

DAVE: Ann, that's fantastic.

ANN: Youngest partner in the firm's history. First woman. Straight track to blah blah blah and all the way up.

DAVE: That's incredible. Why aren't you jumping up and down? We should be out celebrating. If you'd called me, I would've made a reservation. We could be out instead of here eating this.

ANN: I thought you liked this.

DAVE: I do. Mmmm.

ANN: Don't make me come over there and tickle you.

DAVE: No, that would be very undignified for a partner. A New Partner? And so now it's time to start thinking baby names. Well, I guess I owe you a hundred dollars.

ANN: For what?

DAVE: You don't remember?

ANN: Remember what?

DAVE: I guess I shouldn't have brought it up, then. Could've saved a hundred dollars. You really don't remember the bet we made?

ANN: Mmm-mmm.

DAVE: Junior year. Your dorm room. We were pretty drunk, I guess. It was after Sasha's homecoming bash, and you bet me a hundred dollars that you'd make partner before I would. You had absolutely no doubt you'd win. Even though you swore you'd only do it for the good guys and I could do it for anyone. And you were right. You win. (*He takes a hundred-dollar bill out of his wallet and puts it on the table.*)

ANN: You can keep the money, Dave.

DAVE: No, no. A bet's a bet. You win fair and square. (*He writes something on the bill in big letters.*)

ANN: I didn't say yes.

(*Pause*)

DAVE: Why?

ANN: I didn't say no. But I didn't say yes. I said I'd have to talk it over with my husband.

DAVE: Well, I'm touched. Thank you very much. But. So. We talked about it. Don't be ridiculous. Of course I want you to take it. It's what you've always wanted.

ANN: Well, I'm not sure it's what I still want. Things change.

DAVE: You want me to talk you out of it? Why would you possibly want to say no?

ANN: Maybe I want to start a family.

DAVE: We're going to start a family. This is what we've been waiting for.

ANN: But it makes no sense. How are we going to start a family if I'm a partner? What the hell were we thinking?

DAVE: This is a dream come true. You can't start making up excuses to keep yourself from succeeding.

ANN: Can't I just change my mind?

DAVE: We have a plan. It's a good plan.

ANN: We can't change the plan?

DAVE: It's what we've agreed on for our lives. Don't you want that?

ANN: I don't know.

DAVE: Well, if you rejected the offer, what would you want to do?

ANN: I don't know. Quit?

DAVE: What? Jacobson is offering you the opportunity of a lifetime.

ANN: You're not listening to me.

DAVE: No, you're not listening to yourself. I know it's scary to get what you want but, trust me, once you settle into it, you'll see. You'll get the cases you want, you'll get respect. And the rest of our plan will follow.

ANN: How can I know that for sure?

DAVE: I guarantee it. "In times of crisis, always do what you said you would do when you were thinking..."

ANN: Rationally.

DAVE: This is a hell of an offer. It'll take more work, but it'll be worth it, you know that.

ANN: Maybe you're right.

DAVE: We have a good plan. We have a good life.

ANN: I know. You think I just freaked?

DAVE: Yes.

ANN: I guess I got scared.

DAVE: I know, honey.

ANN: Do you think I'm crazy?

DAVE: No. Of course not.

ANN: Alright. I'll do it. (*She takes the hundred-dollar bill and looks at what* DAVE *wrote.*) "For the true winner." Cute.

DAVE: Oh, Ann. I am so proud of you. (*He pours the remainder of the wine into her glass and then his.*) Tomorrow night I'll take you out and we'll celebrate the next phase of our life together.

(ANN *and* DAVE *clink glasses and drink.*)

Scene Two

(ERIC *in* ERIC *and* JULIE's *living room.* ERIC *sings:*)

ERIC: Once upon a time, a few weeks ago, in a faraway kingdom called Seattle.

(JULIE *enters.*)

JULIE: Hi, honey.

ERIC: Welcome home. Did you have a good day?

JULIE: They're all brats.

ERIC: I know, sweetie.

JULIE: Why can't kids listen anymore? Is that so much to ask? Sit. Listen. Don't throw anything. Don't kill anybody. And just maybe in the process you might learn something.

ERIC: Come here.

(ERIC *and* JULIE *kiss.*)

ERIC: Give me your feet.

(JULIE *takes off her shoes, and* ERIC *rubs her feet.*)

JULIE: What did you do today?

ERIC: Well...I've got a lot to fill you in on.

JULIE: Yes?

ERIC: First of all, I went to confirm our registry list. Those people at Williams Sonoma are a nightmare. I was forced to change around a couple of your suggestions, but I think you're going to be very happy.

JULIE: Like what?

ERIC: Nothing major. Only improvements.

JULIE: Oh. O K.

ERIC: Next. I talked to the photographer.

JULIE: And?

ERIC: He agreed with me. We should definitely do the video.

JULIE: You don't think the photos are enough?

ERIC: There's no need for modesty.

JULIE: I just think video cameras are so intrusive. I don't want someone shining bright lights on me through the whole thing.

ERIC: It's totally worth it. I mean you only get a special day like this once in your life and I want everything to be perfect. And I want to remember it perfectly and be able to show it to our kids perfectly.

JULIE: So it has to be on video?

ERIC: You're going to look so beautiful in my mother's dress, and I want it all captured properly. I mean, don't you wish you had a video of your parent's wedding? The last thing we want is to regret not doing it.

JULIE: Alright, if you really think it's worth it, go ahead.

ERIC: That's what I told him. So we're all set.

JULIE: Eric?

ERIC: Yeah?

JULIE: You know how much I appreciate all the work you're doing on the preparations and everything.

ERIC: Not a problem.

JULIE: Well. Thank you. But, and...you know I'm really busy so it's hard for me to put all that work in.

ERIC: I completely understand.

JULIE: But I have to tell you. I mean, since I was a little girl you know, I've had certain visions of how it would be. And, I just want to make sure that I'm included. Does that make sense?

ERIC: Of course. I mean, me too. I have very specific ideas of what our wedding should be. But we've talked, haven't we? We've agreed.

JULIE: Yes, it's just...

ERIC: Very traditional. The whole nine yards. You want that too, don't you?

JULIE: I do...

ERIC: Because I know I do.

JULIE: It's just that sometimes you can be a little overbearing.

ERIC: I can...? I don't mean to be.

JULIE: No. I know. Of course you don't. It's just that I think sometimes you go and make decisions without really consulting me, and I just...it doesn't feel right.

ERIC: About the video?

JULIE: No, it's more of a general thing.

ERIC: I can stop, Julie. Back off I mean.

JULIE: I don't...

ERIC: But I mean, like you said, you don't really have the time....

JULIE: I'm not looking for a solution...

ERIC: And someone has to take care of these things.

JULIE: I know.

ERIC: Perfect example: Your mother called. She needs to invite more people, and is that O K?

JULIE: Who now?

ERIC: Apparently you have an Uncle Phil?

JULIE: I do?

ERIC: Great uncle? Beats me.

JULIE: I've never even met these people.

ERIC: She's your mother, Julie. You weren't here. Someone has to take care of these things.

JULIE: I'm just telling you how I feel.

ERIC: And...O K, well, what can I do to make it better?

JULIE: I don't know.

ERIC: Well...how can I give you want you want if you can't tell me what that is?

JULIE: You don't have to give me what I want all the time. I'm a big girl. You're so eager to please me you... sometimes just, I don't know.

ERIC: No. I what?

JULIE: You treat me like a princess, not a human being. You want so much to make this a perfect "event" up here, that you pay no attention to the "us" down here, and I don't know what that is, what that's about.

ERIC: I'm sorry.

JULIE: You try to make me happy, but then you keep me out of everything. Your eyes are like these impenetrable walls that I can never see through. I never know what you're thinking. I mean, I don't think you do it on purpose....

ERIC: No.

JULIE: But I just thought I should tell you how I felt.

ERIC: No, I'm glad you did. Believe me. It's not easy. I know. And I'm glad you could tell me.

JULIE: I love you, you know?

ERIC: I know. Of course...I love you too.

Scene Three

(MILLER's *house. She sings: Note: when we are in the fairy tale, production values and acting style are more cartoonlike. Not naturalistic*)

MILLER'S WIFE: Once upon a time, a few weeks ago, in a magical kingdom far far away... (*She discovers some papers. Looks at them*) Oh my god! Jumping Jehosafers. Ooooh. This is terrible. Giuseppe. Giuseppe, come in here this instant. Giuseppe, I know you can hear me. Come in here this instant!

(MILLER *enters.*)

MILLER: Yes, my sweet darling wife. What is it?

(MILLER'S WIFE *points to the papers.*)

MILLER: Oh no. You should not look at those. You do not need to concern yourself with our financial matters.

MILLER'S WIFE: Financial matters? What financial matters? You have to have finances to have financial matters. According to this we're broke. Bust. Kaplooey.

MILLER: A woman does not need to concern herself with the accounting. That's a man's job.

MILLER'S WIFE: Man's job my fairy-tale ass. What kind of sexist nonsense is that? I'm tired of all this blatant sexism.

MILLER: What sexism?

MILLER'S WIFE: What sexism? What sexism? What's your name?

MILLER: Why, of course you know my name. You are my wife. My name is Guiseppe Egoist Libidinas Miller.

MILLER'S WIFE: And what's my name?

MILLER: Your name? Why. Your name is...Miller's Wife.

MILLER'S WIFE: Ah-ha. My point exactly. I don't even get a name. Wait? WHOA? Whhhooohhooohhoo. I am having a prophecy. Stand back. I am prophesizing. Mmmmmmmnnn—Centuries from now in a faraway kingdom called New York City (*Insert name of city where show is performing*). In a small theatre called the Ohio (*Insert name of theater*). A place with uncomfortable seating (*Insert own comically disparaging remark*). This point will be uncovered, and young women will feel empowered. Yes. Go my soul sisters of the future. Learn from my plight and be strengthened. Sing. Sing the songs of Woman! (*The trance breaks.*) Whew. Oh. O K. Where were we?

MILLER: What has your prophecy to do with our household finances, my sweet and loving wife?

MILLER'S WIFE: Oh, right, the finances. You can't keep the finances. We're down to our last gold coin.

MILLER: Pshaw. Come now. Things have not gotten so bad. Can you really think we are down to our last gold coin?

MILLER'S WIFE: (*Pulling out a gold coin*) I have one gold coin. What've you got?

(MILLER *sheepishly turns his pockets inside out.*)

MILLER'S WIFE: Exactly.

MILLER: Well, we may not have but one gold coin...but we have other things.

MILLER'S WIFE: Like what?

MILLER: Like our love for each other.

MILLER'S WIFE: That and fifty ducats'll get me a frozen mochaccino, you know what I'm saying?

MILLER: Oh, a frozen mochaccino costs way more than fifty ducats.

MILLER'S WIFE: My point is, we have nothing.

MILLER: We have our apple tree...

MILLER'S WIFE: Giuseppe...

MILLER: Our abundant, flowing apple tree in the backyard.

MILLER'S WIFE: Giuseppe, I'm serious. This is terrible. What are we going to do?

MILLER: I don't know my darling. I tried to keep it from you. I didn't want you to worry. I've tried to make the business work, but times are hard. I can't seem to make ends meet.

MILLER'S WIFE: But what about the mill?

MILLER: The mill is not milling.

MILLER'S WIFE: The mill is not milling?

MILLER: The mill is not milling. The churn is not churning.

MILLER'S WIFE: Ooh. Things are worse than I thought. But don't worry, my sweet. We will find a way to get by.

MILLER: Yes, but how?

MILLER'S WIFE: Perhaps you should go into the forest and chop some wood.

MILLER: Chop some wood? What sort of a cockamamey idea is that? How is chopping some wood going to help our financial troubles?

(MILLER'S WIFE: *bursts into song:*)

MILLER'S WIFE: When times are tough and money's low
As even fairy tales sometimes go
Just grab an ax and head out for the woods.
Forget your fortune dwindling
Go out and get some kindling
And show 'em all you've really got the goods.
You gotta chop chop chop chop chop chop down a tree
There'll be lots of wood for you and for me.
A bundle of faggots and lots of bark.
With enough left over for Noah's ark
You gotta chop chop chop chop chop chop down a
    tree.
You gotta chop chop chop chop chop chop down a
    tree.
Timber!

(*If the song is not used, insert the next line for* MILLER'S WIFE *instead.*)

MILLER'S WIFE: Well. It seems like the sort of thing one might do in a situation like this. (*Pause*) If one lived in a fairy tale.

MILLER: Alright, my darling wife. I am sure you are right. I will go to the forest and chop some wood.

MILLER'S WIFE: Be safe, my font of joy. And be home before dark.

MILLER: Yes, dear. (*He exits.*)

MILLER'S WIFE: Oh boy. Are we fucked.

(MILLER'S WIFE *exits.* MILLER *reenters.*)

MILLER: Well, here I am in the woods. I've got my trusty ax. Guess there's nothing to do but start chopping some wood.

(MILLER *begins to chop some wood. From out of the shadows steps a dark, shadowy figure.*)

DEVIL: Hello, Giuseppe Egoist Libidinas Miller.

MILLER: Hello? Who is that? Do I know you?

DEVIL: Never you mind. I know you. That is all that's important. I understand you've fallen on some hard times.

MILLER: The mill is not milling. The churn is not churning.

DEVIL: Hard times indeed. Terrible shame. Suppose I offered to strike you a bargain that would put an end to your suffering.

MILLER: A bargain? What sort of a bargain?

DEVIL: I will shower you in riches if you but give me what stands in your backyard.

MILLER: (*Thinking aloud to himself*) What stands in my backyard? Hmm? Let's see. What stands in my backyard? Why, nothing stands in my backyard but my apple tree. Can that be all this dark, shadowy man wants from me? My apple tree in exchange for riches? Sounds too easy. Perhaps I should be cautious. (*Pause*)

NAH. What the heck? Riches for an apple tree. (*To* DEVIL) You got a deal!

DEVIL: Very well. In three years' time I will come and take what is mine. (*He retreats into the darkness chortling softly yet evily to himself.*)

MILLER: Wow. What a bargain. I sure am one shrewd negotiator. My wife will be so pleased. I have ended all of our troubles and sorrow. I knew that coming to the forest to chop some wood was a good idea.

(MILLER'S WIFE *comes running onstage.*)

MILLER'S WIFE: Giuseppe. Giuseppe. My goodness. What on earth is happening? Our cupboards are overflowing with game, our trunks and boxes are filled with gold coins, our torn and ragged clothes have turned to velvet. (*She looks at her finger.*) Ahhh! Look, my ring has turned to gold. What can be the meaning of this?

MILLER: My dear and darling wife, listen to me. We are saved. As I was chopping wood I came across a dark and shadowy figure who promised me great wealth if I but gave him what stands in our backyard. Pretty good deal, huh?

MILLER'S WIFE: Oh no! Say it is not so! That dark and shadowy stranger was none other than the devil himself.

MILLER: How do you figure that? A lifetime of riches for an apple tree sounds pretty good to me.

MILLER'S WIFE: What stands in our backyard is our apple tree. Yes. But also in our backyard, sweeping with a willow broom, is...our daughter.

MILLER: No. I've been tricked.

MILLER'S WIFE: When you strike a bargain with the devil you must stay true to your word.

MILLER: And so in three years' time he will come to claim our daughter? We are cursed. What can we do?

MILLER'S WIFE: There is nothing we can do. We must go home and enjoy our last three years of happiness. We must tell our daughter of the terrible fate that awaits her.

MILLER: Oh my God. Can you ever forgive me? I knew not what I was doing.

MILLER'S WIFE: I know, Giuseppe. I know. Come on. There there. Shhh. Let's go home now. Shhh.

MILLER: It seemed like such a good idea at the time.

Scene Four

(ANN *and* DAVE's *house.* ANN *is entering.*)

ANN: Jesus Christ. Fucking animals. Honey? What a day. Fuck me. What time is it? There is no getting out of there. Dave? You're not going to believe the nonsense they threw at me. I have to tell you about this. Are you here? I'm sorry I'm late. Are we still going out? Honey?

(DAVE *enters.*)

DAVE: Hi.

ANN: Hi. Do we have time for a quick drink before we go? I need to unwind. I'm really sorry I'm so late. You have to hear about this day.

DAVE: We're not going out. I cooked.

ANN: You what?

DAVE: I made dinner here. To surprise you.

ANN: No. Oh, honey, I'm so sorry. Is it all ruined?

DAVE: Pretty much.

ANN: Did you make...?

DAVE: Of course.

ANN: Just like for our first anniversary. That is so sexy.

DAVE: We've been married for ten years.

ANN: We're too young to have been married for ten years.

DAVE: And you blew it off.

ANN: I was at work.

DAVE: How could you do that?

ANN: I'm sorry. There was nothing I could do.

DAVE: You could have called.

ANN: I was totally overwhelmed.

DAVE: Don't you care?

ANN: I didn't have a choice.

DAVE: That's it?

ANN: What do you want me to say?

DAVE: I don't know if this is working.

ANN: What?

DAVE: I'm not happy. We need to...I don't know. Do... something.

ANN: If you had gotten promoted, you'd be doing the same thing. Men do this all the time. Are you jealous?

DAVE: It's our anniversary. That means something. You could make the time.

ANN: I'm doing my best. I really am. What do you want me to do? Quit?

DAVE: No.

ANN: Because I will.

DAVE: We have a plan.

ANN: Well then? Why don't we get off the plan?

DAVE: And do what?

ANN: I don't know.

DAVE: No. The plan is a good plan. You know that. I just need you to be better. Better than you are.

ANN: What does that mean?

DAVE: I make the time for you. I take your phone calls.

ANN: I can't be in two places at the same time. I can't juggle everything perfectly. I want more too, you know.

DAVE: Like what? This is a dream come true for you.

ANN: None of this makes sense to me anymore. I'm tired of pretending to be happy instead of actually trying to be happy. Something is...missing.

DAVE: Something like what?

ANN: I don't know.

DAVE: You don't know? Well, you think about it. Think about what you want and what you're willing to do to make it happen. And when you come to some sort of a decision, schedule me into your Filofax and maybe we can talk about it.

(DAVE *exits*. ANN *sings:*)

ANN: If I want to, I can pretend that everything I
      wanted is everything I need.
If I want to, I can pretend that I'm not trapped here
      no indeed.
I can make believe
That I'm really happy
It's a most formidable task.
This is it. This is mine.
Everything is fine.
So why on earth do I gotta ask...

What do you do when you
get what you want? But you
want something other than that
what you got? Which is
what you wanted when you
thought you knew what you
really really wanted in the
first place.
I probably need to get out more.

(If the song is not used, DAVE *should exit and* ANN *should
be left alone on stage for a beat, looking out.)*

Scene Five

*(In the darkness Mendelssohn's wedding march plays. The
lights come up very slowly on* JULIE *in a beautiful, white
wedding dress; she is looking at the ground. As the lights
fade up the music starts to distort. Like an echo of a dream.
As* JULIE *lifts her head we see that she is crying hysterically.
Her face a ruined canvas of smeared makeup. She looks down
at a wrinkled letter she is holding in her hand. She crumples
it in her fist and throws it to the floor as her tears turn
to screams. Lights crossfade to* ERIC, *who is driving on a
highway dressed in a tuxedo. Night. The sound of cars)*
ERIC: Dear Julie.
I'm sorry. But my reasons for leaving are solely due
to my own inadequacies and problems. I need to face
up to my life, and you can't be a part of that. I thought
I could make this work, but I simply can't. Perhaps it
would have been easier and safer to stay, but it would
have been wrong. It probably doesn't seem so to you
now, but believe me—by leaving I am doing you a
huge favor. Please don't try to find me. I am no longer
who I was. I don't expect you to understand or forgive,
but I hope that you will get on with your life and find
the happiness out there you so genuinely deserve.

(Lights up dim on MAIDEN.)

ERIC: As for me, I will always remember your kindness. Your compassion. Your true inner goodness. I don't deserve a place in your heart. Please forget me. Eric.

Scene Six

(MAIDEN, dressed in white, is drawing a circle around herself with chalk in the yard. MILLER and MILLER'S WIFE enter.)

MILLER: Well, my darling wife, it has been exactly three years to the day since I made that hideous bargain. Looks like that wicked devil is not going to claim his reward after all.

MILLER'S WIFE: Oh make no mistake, the devil does not forgo what is his. He will not renege on his bargain.

MILLER: What is it our daughter is doing? Drawing on the ground like that? She looks almost as if she were in a trance.

MILLER'S WIFE: She is guided by the ages. Drawing on the wisdom of those who came before her. She is taking instruction from a faraway time.

MILLER: Mm. Right. Whatever. Anyway...

(DEVIL enters ready to party.)

DEVIL: O K, you deadbeats, Big Daddy's here. Fork over the goods.

MILLER: Oh you wicked, wicked devil. Is there anything I can say to make you change your mind?

DEVIL: Uh. Not likely, but go ahead and give it a shot.

MILLER: Please. Have mercy on us. I was but a poor miller. You duped me. I did not know for what I was bargaining. I love my daughter with all my heart and soul.

DEVIL: Yeah, well, tough luck. Them's the breaks, pops. Look before you leap, know what I mean? Now hand over the broad.

MILLER: She is right over there. Take her if you must.

(DEVIL *sees the* MAIDEN. *Walks over to her. Gets propelled backwards as hard and as far as possible.*)

DEVIL: What gives, pops?

MILLER: Oh she's drawing on the wisdom of...I don't know.

DEVIL: Hmmm. I don't like the looks of this. I got a bad feeling. I think the chick's too clean. Tell you what. Here's the deal. No bathing. Three weeks. Got it.

(MAIDEN *exits.*)

DEVIL: I'll be back. I'm serious about this. No baths. Not even a little, understand? No flippity bippity with a sponge under the pits, huh. No wiggity diggitys with a little splash of water on the back, got it? O K, then. No baths. No water. No nothing. Blah-hah-hah.

(DEVIL *exits.* MILLER *and* MILLER'S WIFE *look at each other then out at the audience.* DEVIL *reenters.*)

DEVIL: O K, it's three weeks later, where the hell's the little chiquita? I'm a busy guy, you know. Don't have time for all this nonsense.

(MAIDEN *reenters. She is as dirty and animal-like as possible.*)

DEVIL: Oh yeah! That's much better. Prime goods.

(DEVIL *crosses towards* MAIDEN. *As he is getting closer* MAIDEN *begins to cry into her hands.* DEVIL *is stopped as if walking into an invisible force field.*)

DEVIL: Oh give me a break. Tears cried by a true heart are like holy water up my ass. Stop crying. Come on. Cut it out now. No more crying.

(MAIDEN *begins to stop crying.*)

DEVIL: Shit. Now with all these tears, her hands are still too clean. We gotta get rid of all the holy water. Miller. Cut off her hands.

MILLER & MILLER'S WIFE: What!?

DEVIL: You heard me. Did I stutter? Cut `em off. Let's go, let's go, let's go, times a wastin'.

MILLER: Surely you cannot ask me to cut off the hands of my daughter.

DEVIL: I can and I will and, if I'm not mistaken, I just did. (*He picks up* MILLER'*s ax.*) Here you are. Let's go. Chop chop. Do the deed.

MILLER: I cannot.

(DEVIL *gets in* MILLER'*s face very seriously.*)

DEVIL: I am not toying with you. Do you understand me? This is not a game. You do not get to decide what you can and cannot do. You made a bargain. Now cut off that little bitch's hands or you die, your wife dies, and this whole fucking village dies.

(MILLER *takes the ax and walks over towards* MAIDEN.)

MILLER: My daughter. I am so sorry. I have some bad news. I'm going to have to chop off your hands. There is nothing I can do.

MAIDEN: You will do what you must.

(MILLER *leads* MAIDEN *to a stump. Puts her hands on it. Raises his ax*)

MILLER: Heaven forgive me.

(He brings the ax down. A flash of blood red. A crashing thud. A brief blackout. Screams in the dark. Lights restore. MAIDEN *has bloody stumps.* MILLER *collapses to his knees.)*

DEVIL: Mine. She's mine. All mine.

*(*DEVIL *runs towards* MAIDEN. MAIDEN *begins to cry. The tears fall on her stumps. The* DEVIL *again hits an invisible force field and is stopped.)*

DEVIL: DAARRGGH. Damn it! Again with those fucking tears. Tears, tears, tears. It's three strikes and I'm out.

MILLER: Three strikes and you're out?

MILLER'S WIFE: If the Devil cannot stake his claim in three attempts, he must relinquish his prize.

DEVIL: Alright, that's it, I'm outa here. But I'll be watching you. Oh yes, make no mistake. I'll be watching. AAARRRGGHHH! *(He exits in a flurry of cacophonous madness.)*

MILLER: My God. His very words have set the woods on fire.

MILLER'S WIFE: My darling, are you alright?

MAIDEN: I am alright, Mother.

MILLER: Boy, I feel like I've aged a hundred years today. My poor daughter. Can you ever forgive me?

MAIDEN: You did what was necessary.

MILLER: Well, at least now he has no claim to you. You have no hands but we can go about rebuilding our lives. We are still very wealthy. Your mother and I can feed you and clothe you and baby you for the rest of your life.

MAIDEN: No, Father.

MILLER: What do you mean no? What more could a child ask?

MILLER'S WIFE: How `bout for a pair of hands?

MAIDEN: This is not the proper life for me. I feel it more fitting that I should become a beggar girl. (*She launches into song:*)
A wandering beggar,
a penniless urchin.
My travels will take me
all over this land
Relying on others,
the kindness of strangers,
won't someone please
lend me a...
Sing hey nonny-nonny,
my parents were wealthy,
will all of my clothing
be tattered and torn?
The life that I led has been
suddenly dumped.
The cards I've been dealt
would suggest I've been trumped.
If you ask where I'm going
I'm bloody well stumped.
This journey I've started
will see me reborn.

(*If the song is not used, simply cut it as well as the* MILLER'S WIFE's *next line.*)

MILLER: Did you hear what she said?

MILLER'S WIFE: She has her mother's voice.

MILLER: Are you out of your mind? What is this, some sort of teenage-rebel-against-your-parents-kind of thing?

MILLER'S WIFE: She must do what she thinks is right.

MILLER: Do what she thinks is right? She should do what her father tells her to do. Sweetheart. We can live in a beautiful castle.

MAIDEN: I do not need a castle, Father.

MILLER: No, but it sure is nice.

MAIDEN: I will go a-wandering and depend on the kindness of others for sustenance.

MILLER: Depend on the kindness of others? Honey, it's a jungle out there. What do you think you're living in, some kind of fairy tale world where people are nice?

(MAIDEN *shoots* MILLER *a look.*)

MILLER: Alright, alright, so you're living in a fairy tale where everyone's nice. O K. Well. If you think that's what's best...go a-wandering.

MAIDEN: Goodbye, Father. (*She kisses him on the cheek.*) Goodbye, Mother (*A hug*) I will miss you both.

(*She exits. Pause. Lights up on* DAVE *entering.*)

MILLER: Rough day.

MILLER'S WIFE: You said it.

Scene Seven

(ANN *and* DAVE's. DAVE *is entering.*)

DAVE: Ann? What a rough day. Jesus Christ. I have to tell you about this. Honey? You here? So get this, right? Remember I told you about Alex and his secretary right? Well, lately, he's been taking these two-hour, three-martini lunches, and when he comes back he's feeling a little...well, frisky, you know? So. Anyway, turns out his wife had decided to give him a little surprise today...

(DAVE *sees a piece of paper on the table. He picks it up and starts to read it. Lights come up on* ANN *driving.*)

DAVE: ...What?

Scene Eight

(*A roadside diner. At lights up* MOE *is cleaning the counter. After a beat* ERIC *enters in his tuxedo and sits at the counter. Note: This scene is a bit dreamlike. Go with it.*)

MOE: Mornin'. Coffee?

ERIC: Yeah.

MOE: Rough party?

ERIC: What? (*Notices his tuxedo*) Oh. This. No. (*He looks at a menu. Looks up*) I'll have...

MOE: Two eggs over easy. Side a bacon. Wheat toast and an O J?

ERIC: Yeah. Um?

MOE: Yes?

ERIC: I have a problem.

MOE: Yes?

ERIC: I don't think I have any money. I...um. I left in a bit of a hurry, and, uh, I can't really go back and...I don't have my wallet on me.

MOE: No money huh?

ERIC: I really need to eat something. Please. I'll mail you a check or something, I swear.

MOE: Hmm. Interesting.

ERIC: Or here. (*He takes off his wedding ring.*) I'll trade you this ring. I'll trade you my ring for two eggs over easy.

MOE: That looks like it's worth a lot of money.

ERIC: It cost a lot of money, that doesn't mean it's worth anything.

MOE: Nah. You keep the ring. Eggs are on the house.

ERIC: Really? Oh, thank you. Thank you very much.

MOE: So, uh. A guy's gotta ask. Why the tux?

ERIC: I left my wife.

MOE: Uh-huh.

ERIC: She's not really my wife.

MOE: Uh-huh?

ERIC: I left her at the altar.

MOE: Oof.

ERIC: I deserve to die.

MOE: Why didn't you want to marry her?

ERIC: What? Oh. I couldn't.

MOE: How come?

(*Pause*)

ERIC: What state am I in?

MOE: You don't know what state you're in?

ERIC: I've been driving.

MOE: What state would you like to be in?

ERIC: I'm headed for New York.

MOE: Where'd you start?

ERIC: Seattle.

MOE: You still got a ways to go. Gotta cross the Mississippi just up ahead.

ERIC: Mmm. This place called Miller's?

MOE: Yup.

ERIC: You Miller?

MOE: Moe.

ERIC: Moe Miller?

MOE: That's me. And you are...?

ERIC: I don't know.

MOE: Not even a name?

ERIC: Eric, I guess. Evan? No. I gotta stay with Eric, I think.

MOE: Pleasure.

ERIC: What?

MOE: I said it's a pleasure to meet you.

ERIC: Oh. Thanks. Same here. (*Pause*) Moe?

MOE: Yo.

ERIC: Am I awake?

MOE: You want to be awake?

ERIC: I want to be dead.

MOE: You're not dead.

ERIC: Moe?

MOE: Yo.

ERIC: I'm gay.

MOE: We serve gays here.

ERIC: What?

MOE: I say you can still have your eggs even though you're gay.

ERIC: Oh. Thanks.

(ANN *enters. Sits at counter*)

MOE: Mornin'. Coffee?

ANN: Yes. Thank you.

(MOE *gets the coffee.*)

MOE: Here you go.

ANN: (*To* ERIC) Would you pass the milk?

ERIC: Sure.

ANN: (*To* MOE) How far to Seattle?

MOE: Seattle? Oh you got a ways to go yet. You still gotta cross the Mississippi up ahead.

ANN: Mmm. Thank you. (*To* ERIC) Rough party?

ERIC: What? (*Notices his tuxedo*) Oh. This. No. I left my wife-to-be at the altar.

ANN: You did that?

ERIC: Yes.

ANN: Just now?

ERIC: Basically.

(ANN *throws her cup of coffee in his face.*)

ANN: Fuck you, asshole.

ERIC: (*Completely calmly*) Ow. You know, that's scalding hot coffee. That really hurts.

ANN: You deserved it. Can I get a refill here?

(MOE *refills* ANN's *coffee.*)

ERIC: I didn't just leave her for no reason, you know.

ANN: Whatever.

ERIC: I did it for her own good.

ANN: Oh I'm sure. You don't just...

ERIC: O K, so I did it for my own good too.

ANN: ...leave people.

ERIC: You don't know what it's like to live a lie. To wake up everyday and pretend to be something you're not.

ANN: I know exactly how that feels.

ERIC: I'm gay.

ANN: Congratulations.

ERIC: I say those words and I expect lightning to strike. The roof to cave in. Doesn't anyone care?

ANN: (*To* MOE) Can I have...?

MOE: Two eggs over easy. Side a bacon. Wheat toast and an O J?

ANN: Yeah.

MOE: Comin' up.

ERIC: Why is it that I say those two words and no one flinches. I'm a completely different person than I was yesterday. Why does nobody see that?

ANN: (*Removing the $100 bill*) Say, can you break a hundred?

MOE: (*Regarding the bill*) Hundred? "For the true winner"? Nah, you keep that. You might need it. Eggs are on the house.

ERIC: I thought if I did this the whole world would end, but this isn't so bad. I should have done this a long time ago. Hey, do you think it's possible to just disappear?

ANN: What?

ERIC: I'm hoping to disappear.

ANN: You want to disappear because you're gay?

ERIC: No, I want to reappear because I'm gay.

ANN: Well, I don't think it's possible.

ERIC: No?

ANN: You can run from your problems, but you can't just disappear. That's retarded.

ERIC: What problems are you running from?

ANN: None of your business.

ERIC: Hey, I told you I was gay.

ANN: I said, none of your fucking business.

ERIC: Sorry. Are you from New York?

ANN: Yeah. Why?

ERIC: That's where I'm headed.

ANN: Turn back now. It's a hell hole.

ERIC: I can't. I'm going to see someone from my past, and if I don't find him I'll...well, I don't know what I'll do. I have to reappear, so I'm still going to disappear, even if you think it's retarded.

ANN: I'm sorry, I didn't mean to be rude.

ERIC: That's O K.

ANN: Sorry about the coffee. I'm just in a bit of a state right now.

ERIC: What happenned?

ANN: I don't know. I...I guess I've been trying so hard to pretend that everything's O K, that it just all came crashing down.

ERIC: Yeah?

ANN: I mean, I'm standing there in Starbucks, right? Reading some article about Bill Gates's house.

ERIC: Oh, brother.

ANN: I know, it sounds stupid, but it suddenly seems like the most incredible place I can possibly imagine. Do you know anything about it?

ERIC: Bits and pieces.

ANN: The house knows what kind of music you like, and it plays it for you wherever you are. The paintings on the wall change to match your taste. The air is always the perfect temperature for your body.

ERIC: Wow.

ANN: It's like some sort of fairy tale castle where the entire house responds to your every desire. I can't imagine that. I have to see it. Touch it.

ERIC: So you just picked up and left?

ANN: I looked down at my coffee, and I looked down at the picture of the house, and the next thing I know I'm in a car headed west.

ERIC: How are you going to get in?

ANN: I don't know.

ERIC: But you had to go.

ANN: I have a great job, and they'll probably fire me. I have a husband whom I love, and I just...abandoned him. But...I just had to...do it anyway. It would have been easier to stay and remain asleep, but I suddenly felt that if I stayed I would die.

MOE: Here are your breakfasts. (*He puts the plates down.*)

(MAIDEN *enters. Her stumps are bound in gauze. The effect of her entrance on* ERIC *and* ANN *is a bit like if Bugs Bunny walked in.*)

MAIDEN: Excuse me, kind people, can anyone assist me? The wind and the road are my new parents. I have no ducats nor gold coins, and I'm a-wandering in search of a new life.

(ERIC *and* ANN *look at each other.*)

(*Blackout*)

END OF ACT ONE

ACT TWO

Scene Nine

(A chamber of the KING'*s.* KING *and* GARDENER *are talking.)*

KING: Tell me this again.

GARDENER: I swear, my Lord, it is the truth.

KING: This maiden had no hands?

GARDENER: None, my Lord.

KING: And she was in my orchard?

GARDENER: That is right, my Lord.

KING: And how did she get into my orchard? How did she pass over the moat?

GARDENER: A spirit.

KING: A spirit. Hmm. How interesting. Hold on one second. *(Speaks into an intercom)* Candy...?? *(Voice: "Yes, Mister King?")* Get Merle in here pronto will ya?

*(*MERLE *enters. He is dressed as a stereotypical wizard.)*

KING: Merle, good to see you.

MERLE: Pardon my appearence, I was just boiling eye of newt. A messy affair. How can I be of assistance, my Lord?

KING: One of my peaches is missing. Now then, tell Merle what you just told me.

GARDENER: I was in the King's orchard, numbering all the peaches as is the wish of my Lord, when I swear that I did see a handless maiden guided by a spirit in white. The spirit did cause the waters of the moat to part, allowing this handless maiden access to the orchard. The maiden tried to bite a peach but the branch was too high. Next thing I knew, the very branch did bend down to meet the handless maiden's lips. She bit of the peach, and then they were gone.

KING: Sounds like a load a hooey to me. What do you say, Merle?

MERLE: What he says is possible, my Lord.

KING: Come now, I think our friend the gardener here got a little hungry, stole a peach, and is now trying to cover up with some fantastical story about handless maidens and spirits in white.

MERLE: That is also possible, my Lord. But what he says does have a ring of truth to mine ear. I suggest that twenty-four hours after the initial sighting we make our way back to the same spot and see if the handless maiden and her spirit guide do come again.

KING: What time did you see them?

GARDENER: (*Looking at his watch*) Doa! We have but five minutes.

KING: Let's go.

(KING, GARDENER, *and* MERLE *cross to another side of the stage. They look offstage. There is a peachtree branch visible.*)

KING: So, is this the spot?

GARDENER: This is it, my Lord.

KING: Well. I don't see anything. You want to amend your story right about now?

MERLE: Look. Off in yonder distance. (*He points offstage.*)

GARDENER: It. It is she. It. It is her. It. It is them.

KING: Well, well, well. Will you lookey here? It is exactly as you say. I was wrong to have doubted you, my faithful gardener. Look. The spirit in white is parting the moat.

GARDENER: They are crossing.

MERLE: They're coming this way.

(MAIDEN *enters and stands beneath the peachtree branch, which magically bends down to meet the* MAIDEN. *She bites the peach.*)

KING: My God. She is the most beautiful woman I've ever seen.

GARDENER: Yeah...if you go for chicks with no hands.

KING: Silence. I must speak to her.

MERLE: Careful, my Lord. We do not know if she is of this world.

KING: Well, how do we find out?

MERLE: Allow me to approach her. (*He walks over towards* MAIDEN.) Do not be afraid, gentle creature, I mean you no harm. Tell me, fair maiden: Are you of this world or not of this world?

MAIDEN: I am of *the* world yet not of *this* world.

MERLE: Hmm, interesting (*He crosses back towards* KING *and* GARDENER, *talking to himself.*) A riddle. Once of *the* world, yet not of *this* world. Once of *the* world, yet not of *this* world.... I have no idea what that means.

KING: Well. Is she human or spirit?

MERLE: She is...both!?

KING: I am enthralled. (*He crosses to* MAIDEN.) I shall not foresake you. I will replace your missing hands with hands of silver. From this day forward I shall care for you. Will you be my bride?

(MAIDEN *looks out to the audience.*)

Scene Ten

(PETER *and* LISA *at a bar.* PETER *is dressed as a* KING, LISA *as a Princess* [MAIDEN]. *Perhaps the other bar from Scene Eleven is visible with* BARTENDER *behind it and* MAX *drinking at it. Perhaps not.*)

PETER: So the magician says to the gardener, "Don't worry, it all went right up my sleeve."

LISA: Oh, brother.

PETER: You don't think that's funny?

LISA: Who told you that one?

PETER: Because he was...

LISA: I get it. Believe me. I get it. Let me guess—

LISA & PETER: Chris.

LISA: What time is it?

PETER: Ten-ten.

LISA: You want to head over?

PETER: We'll be early.

LISA: I thought the party started at nine. (*Pause*) Do we have to stay long?

PETER: We're in—we're out. Soon as I finish my drink, we're off like a prom dress.

LISA: You always say that.

PETER: "Off like a prom dress?"

LISA: No, "we're in—we're out" and then we end up staying forever.

PETER: We won't stay forever, I promise.

LISA: Whatever.

PETER: "Don't worry, it all went right up my sleeve."? You really don't think that's funny?

LISA: Do you mean, should you tell it at the party?

PETER: Yeah.

LISA: No.

PETER: O K.

LISA: This is definitely a costume party, right?

PETER: It's Halloween.

LISA: That doesn't mean it's a costume party.

PETER: It's a costume party.

LISA: I walk in there looking like Snow White and everyone else is in jeans, you're a dead man.

PETER: Relax. We go. We say hello. I kiss Steven's ass. We leave.

LISA: Oh, speaking of ass-kissing, do you think my pecan pie is enough to bring to Thanksgiving?

PETER: Sure.

LISA: Your father's not allergic to pecans, is he?

PETER: No.

LISA: Why do you think he doesn't like me?

PETER: Who?

LISA: Your father.

PETER: He doesn't like anybody.

LISA: He liked your other girlfriends, right?

PETER: More or less.

LISA: So then?

PETER: I don't know, Lisa. I've been trying for thirty years to get him to like me. You want to know why he doesn't like you, ask him.

LISA: Sorry.

(ERIC *enters the bar dressed in his tuxedo, looking around.*)

PETER: Now who's this guy supposed to be? Jimmy Stewart in *It's A Wonderful Life*?

(PETER *and* ERIC *see each other.* ERIC *comes over.*)

PETER: Oh my. Well, well, well. Will you lookey here.

ERIC: Hi.

PETER: Eric. This is my fiancée, Lisa. Lisa this is Eric. A friend of mine from...way back.

ERIC: Hi.

LISA: Hi.

PETER: Gosh, Eric, how long has it been?

ERIC: It's been a while.

PETER: Yes it has. We were actually just on our way out.

ERIC: I understand.

LISA: Halloween party.

ERIC: Yes. You look like a king with his queen.

PETER: Thank you. You look like shit.

LISA: Peter. Rough party?

ERIC: I've been driving.

LISA: Are you alright?

ERIC: Oh, sure. Fine.

LISA: Are you meeting someone here? Do you want to join us?

PETER: Somehow I don't think joining us is quite what he had in mind.

ERIC: No. You know, it's not actually a coincidence that I find you here.

PETER: No?

ERIC: I've been looking for you. It's fairly important, actually. Something personal I need to talk to you about. I'm in a bit of a bind. With um...something you can help me with. If...I could...

PETER: Unfortunately, we really are in a bit of a hurry.

LISA: Don't be rude. He needs to talk to you.

PETER: I'll tell you what, here's my card. Why don't you call me tomorrow and we'll see if we can't straighten things out.

ERIC: I understand.

PETER: (*To* LISA) Come on, we should get going.

LISA: Well, it was nice meeting you.

ERIC: Same here. I'll call you tomorrow.

PETER: You do that.

(PETER *and* LISA *exit.*)

LISA: (*As exiting*) How do you know that guy?

ERIC: Oh boy. Am I fucked.

(ERIC *"swipes" past the bar and as he does it transforms through lights, sound, practicals, acting postures, and/or set pieces into a different bar.*)

Scene Eleven

(MAX *at a bar talking to* BARTENDER.*)*

MAX: So the magician says to the Gardener, "Don't worry, it all went right up my sleeve."

(BARTENDER *laughs.*)

MAX: Give me another one.

BARTENDER: Why don't you slow down? Drinkin' ain't gonna solve your problems.

MAX: Oh, hmm. I'm sorry. I ask you? I don't remember.

BARTENDER: I'm just trying to look out for you, my friend.

MAX: I know. I'm sorry.

BARTENDER: You're gonna have to pick yourself back up. You can't go on like this forever. Listen. I seen this woman in here last night. Asking everyone in the place if they work for Microsoft. Said she'd be back tonight. Maybe you could, uh...you know, give her some inside dope.

MAX: Yeah, maybe.

BARTENDER: Wait `til you see her. Who knows? Maybe it'll be love at first sight.

(ANN *enters.*)

BARTENDER: Burger with fries. Speak of the devil.

(*It is indeed love at first sight.* ANN *sits at the bar. Removes the $100 bill*)

BARTENDER: What can I get for you?

ANN: Gin and tonic.

BARTENDER: I'm out of gin.

ANN: You're out of gin? You're a bar. You can't be out of gin.

BARTENDER: Getcha something else?

MAX: Give her a fuzzy navel.

ANN: No. I don't drink drinks with cute little names. Vodka tonic.

MAX: Give her a fuzzy navel. It's on me.

BARTENDER: Peach Schnapps I got.

MAX: You'll like it.

BARTENDER: Comin' up.

ANN: Thank you. (*To the $100 bill*) Can't seem to get rid of you. (*She puts the $100 bill away.*)

MAX: So what brings you around these parts?

ANN: You work for Microsoft?

MAX: Everyone works for Microsoft somehow. If they don't yet, they will.

ANN: You don't look like a computer geek.

MAX: Computer geek? I don't even have a T V.

ANN: So what do you do?

MAX: I build furniture.

ANN: For Microsoft?

MAX: For the big cheese. For his house. Redwoods are my specialty. He loves the Redwoods.

ANN: Can you get me in there?

MAX: Everyone wants to see the big house. Want to know the truth?

ANN: Yeah.

MAX: It's just a fuckin' house. It's pretty gross if you ask me.

ANN: I don't care. I still need to see it.

MAX: And why should I get you in?

ANN: I left my entire life behind to see this house.

MAX: Gee, that makes sense.

ANN: It doesn't make any sense, but I still have to do it.

MAX: What are you, some kind of freak?

ANN: No, I'm really charming once you get to know me.

MAX: Yeah?

BARTENDER: Here ya go. (*He exits.*)

MAX: What's your name?

ANN: Ann. (*She sips the drink.*)

MAX: I'm Max.

ANN: Nice name.

MAX: Thank you. You married?

ANN: Oh, and here I thought you were just buying me a drink.

MAX: It's a simple question.

ANN: Not always. You married?

MAX: No. No, I'm not married. Was.

ANN: Things didn't work out?

MAX: Huh. No. No, they didn't.

ANN: What happenned?

MAX: I don't really want to talk about it....

ANN: Oh, come on...

MAX: ...tell me about you.

ANN: ...you buy a girl a drink, the least you can do is tell her your life story. It's what all the other boys do.

MAX: Oh, is that how it works?

ANN: Those are the rules. If you wanna play, play fair.

MAX: Well, she...died.

ANN: Oh. I'm sorry. How did she die?

MAX: You don't give up, do you?

ANN: I saw this movie once where the way the cops nailed the killer was because he was the only one who *didn't* ask how the victim had died. So you have to tell or I'll think you think I killed her.

MAX: What?

ANN: Here, look, bartender, give him another one.

MAX: Uh, I think I've had enough.

ANN: Nope. You buy me one. I buy you one. I'll tell you about Dave, if you tell me about...

MAX: Sharon.

ANN: See how easy it is.

MAX: Look...

ANN: Come on, what have you got to lose? Just talk to me. If it doesn't go well, you never have to see me again. But, if it does go well...you show me the house.

MAX: O K. Fine. I was uh...out of state. Doing a fair. That's what I did before I started working for the big cheese. And uh...some guy broke into our house and uh...killed...her. Killed her then...raped her.

(ANN *starts to laugh.*)

MAX: What the hell's so funny?

ANN: (*Still laughing*) It's not, it's not funny. God, that's awful.

MAX: Ha ha ha. Maybe this isn't such a good idea. (*He starts to go.*)

ANN: No, wait. Please don't go. I'm sorry. I didn't know. I was just shocked I didn't mean any offense, and...here, the drinks are on me. (*She puts the $100 bill on the bar.*)

MAX: I haven't even said her name out loud in a year and you think it's funny?

ANN: Not funny. Ridiculous. Absurd. How can you make sense of something like that? But if you can't laugh...I don't know.

MAX: It hurts.

ANN: I know. But it's not like "not talking about it" is gonna make it go away.

MAX: No.

ANN: You know, when I started driving out here I thought I must be out of my mind. Throwing everything away on what seemed like a whim. But I think it's actually a lot worse to stay trapped in what you know. Sometimes you just need to take a chance.

MAX: Would you throw that drink in my face if I told you you were beautiful?

ANN: No.

MAX: You're very beautiful.

ANN: You're very beautiful too. You, uh, chat up all the girls in this place?

MAX: No. I don't know how to talk to girls. I married her when I was nineteen.

ANN: Who?

MAX: My wife.

ANN: Who?

MAX: ...Sharon.

ANN: You do O K.

MAX: Thanks. You like that fuzzy navel?

ANN: Peachey. Sweet.

MAX: Yeah.

ANN: Max?

MAX: Yeah?

ANN: Do you really build furniture for that house?

MAX: Nope.

ANN: I didn't think so.

MAX: Sorry. You want to keep talking to me?

ANN: Of course.

MAX: Ann?

ANN: Yeah?

MAX: I really build furniture for that house.

(As the lights change, MAX *and* ANN *exit.* MESSENGER *enters.)*

Scene Twelve

(A MESSENGER *running in the forest.)*

MESSENGER: I hate this fuckin' war. This fucking war. Gimme that land. Gimme those ducats. *(She picks up the $100 bill.)* Fight fight fight fight fight. *(She pockets the bill.)* King's needed on the battlefield. Queen's at home with his mother. And I gotta run around like a jerk, delivering messages back and forth, back and forth, always bloody back and forth. I'm just trying not to get killed. Aw, geez. My friggin' feet are killing me. I wonder if I could just lay me down by the side of this here brook. Just for a minute. You know—rest the old weary eyes. *(She lays down. Closes eyes. After a beat bolts upright)* I am not going to sleep, though. Nuh-uh. Too much important work to do. *(She goes to sleep.)*

(From out of the darkness steps the DEVIL.)*

DEVIL: Well well well. Let's just see what we have here. *(He takes the message and reads it.)* Dear King. Your

beautiful wife has given birth to a beautiful baby boy.
Glorious news. Love, Mother. Nyah-Nyah-Nyah. Foo!
So... The Handless Bitch has mothered a child. Well.
We'll just see about that. (*He takes out a pen and scrawls
on the message.*) New new new, hoo hoo hoo, hubba
hubba doo doo. Love, Mother. (*He replaces message and
exits.*) Wake up!

MESSENGER: (*Awakening*) Wha-? Who? Not sleeping.
Oh, sheesh. O K. I feel better. Now then. Gotta get this
message to the King.

(MESSENGER *starts walking. Meets up with the* KING.)

MESSENGER: Hello, my Lord. I come bearing news from
the castle.

KING: News from the castle? Oh, goodey-goodey. Is it
about my wife? I cannot wait to see.

(MESSENGER *hands* KING *the message, which* KING *reads
aloud.*)

KING: Dear King. You wife has given birth to a child
which is half dog. Seems that in your absence she has
been copulating with the beasts in the woods. Please
advise. Love, Mother. Oh my. Well, this is terrible
news. What am I to do? Can this really be so? My wife?
Think think think think think. Messenger. Send back
the following message. (*He scrawls a message and hands
the new message to the* MESSENGER.) Be sure you do not
dally. Move with great haste. Over hill and valley.
There is no time to waste.

MESSENGER: No my Lord!

(KING *exits.* MESSENGER *heads back towards the castle.*)

MESSENGER: "Yes, my Lord; no, my Lord. Do this. Do
that. Hurry up." Fuck you! As soon as I save enough
gold coins, I'm blowin' this dead-end job.

(DEVIL *sticks his head out of the shadows.* MESSENGER *lets out a big yawn.*)

MESSENGER: Aw, gee, I'm suddenly feeling very sleepy again. I could swear I just rested mine eyes. (*Another yawn. Sits*) Maybe I'll just sit down for a second and, you know...just for a second. (*She falls asleep.*)

(DEVIL *approaches and reads the message.*)

DEVIL: Well, well, well. Let's just see what little Kingy has to say about his predicament. (*Reading*) Dear Mother. Can your news be true? Please send confirmation. Love, King. Oh, no, no, no. This will not do at all. Please allow me. (*He scrawls on the message.*) Hubbidy-hubbidy-hubbidy-hubbidy wicka-wacka-woo. There, that's much better. (*He returns the message to the* MESSENGER *and exits.*) Wake up.

MESSENGER: Oh boy. I feel much better. Alright now. On with my journey. Back to the castle.

(MESSENGER *continues on. Runs into the* KING'S MOTHER—CRONE.)

CRONE: Messenger, you've returned at last. What the devil took you so long?

MESSENGER: Not sleeping. No! Not me. No way. No, ma'am. Nuh-uh. No sleeping for me.

CRONE: Did the King send back a reply?

MESSENGER: You bet your britches he did.

(MESSENGER *hands* CRONE *the message.*)

CRONE: (*Reading*) Mother. Kill the child and the woman. Immediately. Love, King. P S: Please be sure to cut out and keep the woman's eyes and tongue for confirmation. (*Pause*) Heavens to Murgatroy. What am I to do? I must consult...my book. (*She exits.*)

MESSENGER: Oh no, no, no. Not again. She's gonna send me out there again, I know it. I just know it. Oh, this is ridiculous. Can't we be done with this? I mean, did I mention that there's a fuckin' WAR going on out there? That's dangerous. Geez. Why can't things be easy like they are in the real world?

Scene Thirteen

(ERIC *outside* PETER's. ERIC *enters, looking at a business card. He goes to ring a doorbell. Stops. Straightens up. Closes his eyes.* PETER *enters from behind him. Note: This scene is a fantasy, feel free to go over the top.)*

PETER: Hello.

ERIC: Hi.

PETER: That was quite a little scare you gave me.

ERIC: I know, I'm sorry. But I had to talk to you.

PETER: So. Talk.

ERIC: I want to come back.

PETER: Really?

ERIC: I've been so miserable without you. The times we had together, I mean...it's what makes life worth living, don't you think?

PETER: Go on.

ERIC: I miss you so desperately. I threw everything away to come back to you.

PETER: Well, I must say, this is very touching. Who wouldn't want the lover who spurned him to come crawling back on his knees.

ERIC: Consider me begging then. (*He breaks into song:*)
I have nothing
Not a dollar
Just a car
And a tux

And a credit card
For gasoline
Which sort of counts as a couple of bucks
And I want to be
The me I am
Whenever I'm with you
I'm sorry
I'm so sorry
For what I put you through
Everybody else's life is normal
Everybody seems to have a clue
And I want to be
The me I am
Whenever I'm with you.

(If the song is not used, cut it, and replace with the next line for ERIC:*)*

ERIC: I have nothing. Not a dollar. Just a car and a tux. I want to be me again. The me I am when I'm with you.

PETER: Things certainly haven't been the same for me since you left.

ERIC: They haven't? Me neither. I don't care how much time has passed, this is the only life I want.

PETER: What happened to what's her name?

ERIC: Julie. I left her.

PETER: I wish I had the courage to leave Lisa.

ERIC: You do. We can start over. I made a mistake, but I'm back.

PETER: I wouldn't even know where to start.

ERIC: One step at a time.

PETER: You make it sound like a twelve-step program.

ERIC: It is what it is. Just start with a kiss.

PETER: Just a kiss?

ERIC: That's where we start. We'll see where it goes from there.

PETER: Alright.

(ERIC *approaches* PETER *cautiously. They kiss. Passionately.*)

PETER: I am so fucking in love with you.

(PETER *freezes as* ERIC *addresses the audience.*)

ERIC: Oh, God, let's hope.

(ERIC *walks around the still-frozen* PETER *and rings a doorbell.*)

Scene Fourteen

(ANN *and* MAX *at* MAX's. *They are a couple.*)

MAX: So...what did you think of the house?

ANN: I still don't understand why it took three weeks before I could see it.

MAX: Security clearances. It's not easy to get in there, you know.

ANN: Uh-huh.

MAX: And, besides, I needed a carrot at the end of the stick.

ANN: Oh, I think you're enough of a carrot.

(ANN *and* MAX *kiss.*)

MAX: So. Answer the question. What did you think of the house?

ANN: Want to know the truth?

MAX: Yeah.

ANN: It's just a fuckin' house. It's pretty gross, if you ask me.

MAX: Told you.

ANN: It was just so disappointing. I mean, there I am. The temperature is perfect. I'm staring at...a Georgia O'Keefe, listening to...Aretha Franklin, everything's perfect, and I still feel like shit. I still feel like there's a hole in my life. I don't know what I thought it would give me.

MAX: A house like that can't give you anything. A perfect house is one you build with your own hands. And you know what the secret ingredient is?

ANN: What?

MAX: Love.

ANN: Build your own house?

MAX: Build you a house. For us. I have some land that I had been thinking I was going to build on. But...after Sharon died I just sort of...stopped. But now I think it's time to start building again.

ANN: Really? Don't you think...

MAX: I mean, I don't want to move too fast, and it would take some time anyway, but I think I can do it. Me and Ted together, we can make just about anything.

ANN: Oh, my god, that is about the sexiest thing I've ever heard. I love that.

MAX: Are you sure?

ANN: Build a home? For me. For us. Build a future.

MAX: That's the idea.

ANN: I came out here looking for a fantasy castle and now I get Prince Charming to go with it?

MAX: I'll do my best.

ANN: What would I do out here if I stayed?

MAX: We have lawyers in Seattle too, you know.

ANN: But maybe I don't want to be a lawyer anymore.

MAX: Then be whatever you want.

ANN: Hmm, so let's say I wanted to be a potter.

MAX: That would be great.

ANN: A chef.

MAX: I love to eat.

ANN: A gardener.

MAX: The choice is yours.

(*The phone rings. Again*)

ANN: Do you want to get that?

MAX: No. I want to take you upstairs...and lay you down on the bed I built...and, even if only for an hour or so, do all we can to forget everything we ever knew.

ANN: O K. You go upstairs. I'll be up in a minute.

MAX: You O K?

ANN: I just want to be alone in a world of possibilities for a second.

(MAX *exits.* ANN *closes her eyes. The phone is still ringing. She opens her eyes.*)

ANN: What am I doing?

(*An answering machine beep...*)

Scene Fifteen

(Three separate areas. DAVE, JULIE, MILLER. *Lights up on* DAVE. *A "/" indicates where an overlap begins.)*

DAVE: Hello? I'm sorry, "Max", for taking up space on your machine, but I'm trying to reach my wife. Ann, I was hoping to get you, but what the hell?

(Lights come up on JULIE *reading a letter on pink stationery.)*

JULIE: My dearest Eric. You certainly did a great job. The gifts from Williams Sonoma made for fabulous returns, my great Uncle Phil kept saying, "buck up, it just means more alcohol for the rest of us", and the video of me crying is particularly moving.

(Lights come up on MILLER *reading a letter.)*

MILLER: Dear my darling daughter Maiden. Why don't you ever write to your mother and me? We sit around and wonder if we will ever hear from you again. / You're probably...

DAVE: You're probably out, I don't know, doing whatever people do for fun out there. But /I have to tell....

JULIE: I have to tell you I was devastated. I felt like a nothing and a nobody. Watching you ride off into the sunset while I am left cleaning up your mess. / I still feel...

MILLER: I still feel pretty guilty about what happened. I mean, even though I was tricked by the Devil himself, I still feel bad. / I want...

DAVE: I want you to come home to me, Ann (this is so weird, talking into a tape). I love you and...and I miss you, and...I don't know what the hell else am I supposed to say. You're everything to me, you know. / I mean...

MILLER: I mean between you, me, and the candlestick, things between your mother and me are not as good as they used to be, and believe it or not I even miss the mill. I miss milling. It was a lot of hard work, but I was happy. / Because of this...

JULIE: Because of this, my depression has led my work to suffer tremendously. I couldn't sleep or concentrate. Eric, I knew you were gay. Or wanted to be gay. I just wanted us to be happy together. But if not I will find a way to be happy without you as I hope you are without me. / I think...

DAVE: / I think...

MILLER: I think all the time about what it would be like if you were still here. I think it would be a lot better. All I have to console myself with is more money than I could have ever possibly imagined. And I mean, O K, that's not so bad. But I would trade everything to have you back. / If I cannot...

JULIE: If I cannot forget you, I can at least move forward without you. No matter what, there's a comfort in knowing that we are always moving forward towards something.

DAVE: But we can work things out, I know we can. I'm nothing without you. I'm... Please. I'm so fucking miserable. The apartment just feels so empty. I know it's hard for me to bend but I need you. You're my partner. In everything. You...you make me... You... Oh, God. I mean, I'm pretty fine actually. I mean, I'm O K. You know. No one needs to know what's inside. Just... keep...

(An answering machine beep)

DAVE: Hello? Hello? No.

(Lights out on DAVE, who exits.)

JULIE: I've done all I can to try to find you, but apparently you cover your tracks very well. And so I send these thoughts out into the ether in the hopes they'll reach you. Sleep well, my forsaken prince. Live in peace. Love, Julie.

(JULIE *looks over the letter and then rips it in half and in half again. She exits. As she does the* MESSENGER *enters and picks up the pieces of her letter while on route to the* MILLER.)

MILLER: Anyway. I wonder about you. I wonder if you are happy. I sure do hope that you are. Love, your father, Giuseppe.

(MILLER *hands his letter to* MESSENGER.)

MESSENGER: There's no address on this letter.

MILLER: I know. Just tell me you'll deliver it.

MESSENGER: I'll deliver it.

Scene Sixteen

(ERIC *and* PETER *at* PETER'S).

PETER: So, you're telling me you threw everything away just to find me.

ERIC: Yes.

PETER: Where have you been sleeping?

ERIC: My car. I haven't eaten much. I...forgot my wallet.

PETER: Well, I must say, this is very touching.

ERIC: I have nothing. Not a dollar. Just a credit card for gas to get me here. I'm here. Without you I have literally nothing. A car and a tux.

PETER: I'm not sure that was your most prudent move.

ERIC: Let me back in. I'm sorry. Please. I'm... I've been in Seattle living out some bizarre version of normalcy that I can't stand. I want to be me again. The me I am when I'm with you. We're so good together but... I couldn't see that.

PETER: No, you couldn't.

ERIC: I thought our relationship was some glorious game I was allowed to play until I had to go back to real life. But this is the only real life I want.

PETER: Look. Stop, O K? I thought having you crawl back to me on your knees would feel good, but I don't want to hear this anymore. I'm happy, alright? Happy with Lisa. Happy with the way things are. The best thing you can do is leave.

ERIC: Are you happy? Or are you pretending to be happy? Because I pretended for a long time. It's easy to convince yourself.

PETER: I think you put it real well. It was a nice game we had. But at this point, and I'm sorry if this hurts you, but you're just not worth what I'd have to go through to be with you.

ERIC: None of that matters. Throw all that extraneous crap out.

PETER: Oh, like you did. Mister big responsible man, just walking away from his problems. Twice.

ERIC: Tell me, what's so great about Lisa?

PETER: None of your business.

ERIC: That's compelling. One thing. Just tell me one thing you love about her.

PETER: She...loves my jokes and I love to make her laugh. That's two.

ERIC: Fine. And now one thing about me.

PETER: You left me.

ERIC: One good thing that you love.

PETER: Loved.

ERIC: Love.

PETER: It's too late.

ERIC: Say it. Say what you used to say. Say it and I'll leave.

PETER: ...I love your eyes.

ERIC: Come on. Say it.

PETER: I love the way your whole being is transparent in your eyes.

ERIC: Go on.

PETER: I always know what you're feeling.

ERIC: And what am I feeling right now? Look in my eyes and tell me.

(ERIC *and* PETER *stare into each other's eyes.*)

PETER: I love Lisa. And I'm going to marry Lisa. Look, I'm sorry that you threw away your life for some entitlement fantasy that you could waltz in here and win me back, but you're too late.

ERIC: Kiss me.

PETER: No.

ERIC: Give me one kiss and try to tell me there's no magic left between us.

PETER: I'm not interested anymore.

ERIC: One kiss. Come on. I came all this way. One kiss and I'll go.

PETER: Fine.

(PETER *goes to kiss* ERIC. ERIC *grabs hold. There is magic. At length* PETER *stops.*)

PETER: Now get the fuck out of my life.

Scene Seventeen

(CRONEY *and* MAIDEN *in the castle.* MAIDEN*'s hands are silver. She holds the baby.*)

MAIDEN: I cannot believe the King would wish to have me killed.

CRONEY: It does seem most strange and yet his instructions are as clear as day. He even confirmed them.

MAIDEN: I don't understand. Before he went to war he was so wonderful. Giving me these hands of silver. Making me the Queen. Fathering my child. Can war have turned him into so vile a monster?

CRONEY: I don't know.

MAIDEN: What are we to do?

CRONEY: Well, certainly I will not have you killed. I have a plan. I have sacrificed a doe and saved the eyes and tongue as proof of your death. That should satisfy the King.

MAIDEN: And what am I to do?

CRONEY: You, I'm afraid, must a-wander.

MAIDEN: Again?

CRONEY: The king must not find you alive.

MAIDEN: But how am I to wander without my spirit guide?

CRONEY: Your spirit guide will be with you. She is inside you now. Do not be afraid.

MAIDEN: But I will miss you so. And the King.

CRONEY: I know, my sweet maiden. I shall miss you too. But there is no other way. Now take the baby and be gone.

(CRONEY *and* MAIDEN *hug.*)

MAIDEN: Alright. You know best. If you think it is right, I will do it. Goodbye.

CRONEY: Goodbye, fair maiden.

MAIDEN: Thank you for all of your kindness.

CRONEY: No problem.

MAIDEN: Think of me.

CRONEY: Go now.

(MAIDEN *exits.*)

CRONEY: Well. What is there to do but wait for the war to end and the King to return?

(KING *enters.*)

KING: Well, the war is over and I'm back. Hello, Mother. Where is my lovely wife?

CRONEY: As you commanded I have had her killed.

KING: What!?

CRONEY: She and the baby. Look. Here are the eyes and tongue as proof.

KING: Oh my God, that's disgusting! This is awful.

CRONEY: But it is just as you wished.

KING: What are you talking about?

CRONEY: Your letter.

KING: My letter said to care for my wife and the baby despite the fact that the baby is half dog.

CRONEY: Half dog. What are you talking about?

KING: That's what it said in your letter.

CRONEY: Oh no. Oh no. Something has gone terribly wrong. Your son is not half dog. It is the Devil's work. He has switched our letters to each other with these wicked and horrible lies.

KING: And to grave consequences. Now my wife and son are killed.

CRONEY: No, my Lord. I did not actually have them killed.

KING: What are you saying now?

CRONEY: I faked their deaths. These eyes and tongue are of a sacrificial doe. I could not bear to see them killed.

KING: Oh, joy! This is wonderful. Mother, you are ever so clever. So then, where are my wife and son?

CRONEY: I thought you wanted them killed so I dared not have them here upon your arrival. They have gone a-wandering.

KING: Well, where have they gone a-wandering to?

CRONEY: I do not know. They are gone for good.

KING: Oh, no, they're not. I will find them. I will search as long as the sky is blue. (*He breaks into song:*)
Though the sky may burn with lightning
And the Devil's had his say
I swear on my crown
I won't let them down
Look out, I'm on my way.
They've gone I know not where
It's far too much to bear
I feel the need to share
So beware!
Though the odds are stacked against me
In the end I'll win the day
You see, here's the thing

I'm the Goddamned King!
Look out, I'm on my way!

(If the song is not used, replace the KING's *prior line with the following one:)*

KING: Oh, no, they're not. I will find them. I will search long and hard. I will go without food and drink. I will search as long as the sky is blue. I don't care how long it takes. I will find my wife and son.

Scene Eighteen

*(*MAX's*)*

MAX: Halloooo? I'm getting tired of waiting up here by myself. *(He enters in boxers.)* I'm starting to get hungry. We just might have to break out the chocolate sauce. Are you hiding? Are we playing a little game of hide and seek? O K. I'm coming after you. And when I find you, you're mine, all mine. You can't hide forever. I'm going to catch you. Come out, come out wherever you are. *(He finds a piece of paper. He reads it.)*

(Lights up on ANN *driving.)*

MAX: Oh, no, you don't.

Scene Nineteen

*(*MOE's *roadside diner.* MOE *is cleaning the counter. Enter* MAIDEN *with her silver hands.)*

MOE: Mornin'. Coffee?

MAIDEN: Coffee? What is coffee?

MOE: Skip it. What can I do you for?

MAIDEN: Well, kind sir, I have been wandering long and far. I need a place to cure my weariness, and I wonder if you might be the proprietor of Moe and Flo's bed and breakfast.

MOE: That's me. Moe Miller. Proprietor of Moe and Flo's. Rooms are right upstairs. If you're interested, the wife'll be happy to accommodate you.

MAIDEN: Thank you, kind sir. You are most kind indeed.

MOE: Say there, uh, just one question: Aren't you the Queen?

MAIDEN: Why, I am the Queen, indeed. How would a man such as yourself know that?

MOE: Oh, I keep up on those things. Anyway, stay as long as you like. Entrance is right around back.

MAIDEN: Thank you. You are so very kind. (*She exits.*)

(*After a beat* ERIC *enters.*)

MOE: Mornin'. Coffee?

ERIC: Thank you.

MOE: Say. You look awfully familiar to me.

ERIC: I came in here once a while ago.

MOE: Yeah. I knew it. I never forget a face. You were gonna give me that nice ring, right?

ERIC: That was me.

MOE: So, let me see. You were gay. That right? Looking for your boyfriend or something.

ERIC: I found him.

MOE: Congratulations.

ERIC: Turns out he has no interest in me.

MOE: Ouch. So what are you gonna do?

ERIC: I don't know. I can't go forwards and I can't go back. I need to clear my head, you know?

MOE: Time seems to have a very magical effect for that sort of thing.

ERIC: I need a place to focus. Collect my thoughts.

MOE: Well, listen, if I'm not buttin' in too much, I know the perfect place for you.

ERIC: Where?

MOE: Moe and Flo Miller's Bed & Breakfast. Right upstairs. Perfect place to clear your head.

ERIC: Really? What's so special about it?

MOE: Well. That's kinda hard to put into words. Let's just say that fairy tales can come true. It can happen to you. If...

(ANN *enters.*)

MOE: Oh. Mornin'. Coffee?

ANN: Yes, please. (*She notices* ERIC.) Hey, don't I know you from somewhere?

ERIC: You do look familiar. But I don't...

ANN: I threw coffee in your face.

ERIC: Oh yeah. Hey. How you doing? You were running away as I remember.

ANN: Yup. That was me. Still am, I guess.

ERIC: Good thing I'm not the one looking for you, huh? What are you running away from again?

ANN: Well, I was running to Seattle and now I'm running from Seattle.

ERIC: That sounds like a lot of running.

MOE: Still running huh? Still trying to find something "out there".

ANN: Yeah. I guess. What about you? I thought you were going to disappear...reappear?

ERIC: Well, I was heading to New York to find my old boyfriend, but...

ANN: Oh, right, you're gay. That was like a big deal to you as I recall.

ERIC: Right, right. I finally make the big decision to be true to myself, but I couldn't get Peter to do the same thing.

ANN: I'm sorry.

ERIC: Once upon a time I had a great life with him, you know, but I couldn't see it. And now it's too late. I can't go back to him.

ANN: Do you think it's always too late to go back?

ERIC: I don't know.

MOE: "Always". So black and white.

ERIC: Meantime, I crushed my fiancée.

ANN: The one you left at the altar?

ERIC: I mean, I guess I should go back and tell her I'm sorry, right? Ask her to forgive me.

ANN: I wouldn't do that if I were you.

ERIC: Why not?

ANN: You've already hurt her enough.

ERIC: But I need to know that she's alright and that it's O K for me to move on. I need to start a new chapter, you know? Again and again and as many times as it takes until I get it right. I mean, if I can't have a happy ending I can at least try for a new beginning, right?

ANN: So forgive yourself. Know that what you did was wrong and get on with your life. She'll be O K.

ERIC: How can I be sure?

ANN: I don't think you can be sure.

ERIC: Well...thanks. Good luck. It was good running into you. I was just going to see about a room.

ANN: A room? I sure could use a good place to sack out for a couple of nights.

MOE: Might I recommend Moe and Flo's Bed and Breakfast. Accommodations fit for a Queen.

ANN: Really? Thank you. Thank you very much.

MOE: Right on out through there.

(ANN *and* ERIC *exit. Beat.* MAX *enters.)*

MOE: Mornin'. Coffee?

MAX: Thank you.

MOE: Know what you'd like?

MAX: Yeah, um...

MOE: Stack a pancakes. Side a bacon. Maple syrup gently rolling over the top of yer cakes and just... kissing yer side of bacon?

MAX: Yeah. That'd be great.

MOE: Comin' up.

MAX: Do you have a kid?

MOE: Me? Yeah, sure.

MAX: How old?

MOE: Two.

MAX: What's his name?

MOE: Moe.

MAX: Moe Miller?

MOE: That's me.

MAX: Isn't that him?

MOE: That's little Moe.

MAX: Gotcha. Say, uh, how far am I from New York?

MOE: Where'd you start?

MAX: Seattle.

MOE: I'd say you're about halfway.

MAX: Thanks.

MOE: Still gotta cross the Mississippi up ahead. Why you headed to New York?

MAX: I'm looking for this woman. We had this great electricity together, and then she suddenly...left out of the blue.

MOE: And you want to find her, tell her you love her, and have a nice happy, fairy tale ending.

MAX: Yeah. I guess I kind of do. You think that's stupid?

MOE: No. Not at all. We all want that, don't we?

MAX: I quit drinking. That's a good sign, right? I mean for our future together.

MOE: Good as any.

MAX: I hope I can find her.

MOE: Oh, you'll find her. True love always wins out in the end. If...

(DAVE *enters and sits at the counter.*)

MOE: Mornin'. Coffee?

DAVE: Fuck me, yes. Please.

(MOE *pours the coffee.*)

DAVE: Thank you. Would you pass the milk? Can you tell me how far I am from Seattle?

MOE: Where'd you start?

DAVE: New York.

MOE: I'd say you're about halfway. Still gotta cross the Mississppi up ahead.

MAX: I'm from Seattle.

DAVE: My fucking car just broke down.

MAX: Really? What's wrong with it? Maybe I could take a look at it.

DAVE: Are you a mechanic?

MAX: No, but I'm pretty handy.

MOE: Do you know what you'd like?

DAVE: Um... Oh, I don't know, I guess I'll have...

MOE: Stack a pancakes. Side a bacon. Maple syrup gently rolling over the top of yer cakes and just... kissing yer side of bacon?

DAVE: Yeah, that would be great.

MAX: Why are you going to Seattle?

DAVE: To find my wife.

MAX: Really, I'm going to New York to find my girlfriend.

DAVE: Small world.

MAX: You think she'll come back? Your wife?

DAVE: She has to.

MAX: I'm sure she will. True love always wins out in the end. Right, Moe?

MOE: Oh, boy.

MAX: What's she doing in Seattle?

DAVE: I don't know. She's confused. I'm confused. She was one of the most brilliant lawyers I've ever seen, I mean, if she wants to be a potter or whatever, that's fine, but she doesn't belong out there. She belongs with me. It's just a fact.

MAX: Hmm...well, maybe she needed to leave to appreciate what she already had. (*He takes the letter out of his pocket.*)

DAVE: Mmm, maybe so. (*He takes the letter out of his pocket.*) Maybe I needed her to go to see how much I need her to stay. My name's Dave by the way.

MAX: Yeah. I know.

DAVE: I'm sorry...?

(KING *enters, carrying a "Missing" poster.*)

KING: Excuse me, kind people. I'm looking for my wife and son, who have run away due to a grave misunderstanding. I have been searching high and low for nigh on seven years. I would be most grateful for any information.

MOE: Pardon my asking, but...aren't you the King?

MAX & DAVE: The King!?

KING: Why, yes. I am the King.

MOE: My Lord, if you'll pardon my saying so, you look terrible.

KING: I have been wandering for nigh on seven years in search of my wife.

MOE: Your wife the Queen?

KING: But of course my wife the Queen. Who else?

MOE: But, my Lord, what incredible fortune. Why, she's...

(MAIDEN *enters, carrying her silver hands in her real hands.*)

MAIDEN: It is a miracle! My hands have grown back. First as baby hands, then as little girl hands, and now miraculously restored as my full-grown hands.

KING: My Queen?

MAIDEN: Uh...no. Must be someone else. Me not Queen. Queen killed and...uh, eyes poked out. Confirmation. Tongue too. Yech. Me not her. Nuh-uh.

KING: No, no, my Queen. My mother told me everything. It was all a grave misunderstanding. The work of the Devil.

(ANN *enters.*)

KING: I have searched high and low for you for nigh on seven years. At last we are together again.

MAIDEN: Oh. Thank goodness. You found me and now we can be together. Joy at last. I will introduce you to your son and we shall live happily ever after.

ANN: Oh...my...God.

MAX: Ann.

DAVE: Ann. Ann? How do you know my wife?

ANN: Dave, Max. Wait.

MOE: Gentlemen, please.

DAVE: You're not the guy with the furniture and the big dog!?

MAX: Look, I...

ANN: Boys, don't.

KING: Cease!

(DAVE *and* MAX *cease.*)

KING: Now then, young maiden, these two princes are obviously willing to compete for your hand. But only you can decide who is the proper suitor. Only you can determine what will bring you happiness.

(ANN *looks them both over. Surveys the situation*)

ANN: Oh, God. Why can't I have my happy ending handed to me like you two?

KING: Handed to us?

MAIDEN: That's not funny.

KING: You think this was easy? I have searched high and low for nigh on seven years. I have gone without sleep. Without food nor drink. I'm pretty fuckin' tired and hungry. No one gave this to me. I sacrificed. I made this happen. I had to outwit the Devil himself. Jiminey, I hate it when people make these things seem easy.

ANN: O K. Fine. But that's just you. What about her?

MAIDEN: Me? I had my hands cut off. I had to leave my family. I was almost killed by the King. I have been wandering for years and years guided by nothing but faith. I have suffered beyond belief.

ANN: But the last time I saw you you had nothing, now you have everything. You found your Prince Charming. A man willing to sacrifice for you. A man who truly loves you.

KING: And what do you have before you? Prince number one...

MAX: Ann, we were headed for such a wonderful life. Building the house. Don't you want that? How could you throw that away to go back to something that wasn't making you happy?

KING: Prince number two...

DAVE: Ann, I have always loved you. Since we were... kids, really. I want you back so desperately. We just have to make sure that we don't get complacent or take each other for granted. We've been married for ten years. We have to respect that and try again.

KING: Maiden...

ANN: I don't think you can do it. It's too much work.

DAVE: Then we'll make it our life's work.

ANN: What about the plan?

DAVE: We'll throw out the plan. I don't care about the job or the apartment or New York.

MAX: It's bullshit.

DAVE: I'll throw it all away if I have to.

MAX: Habits are too hard to break.

DAVE: I came running after you. Just picked up and left. We need each other.

MAX: You'll end up right back where you were, you know that.

DAVE: Please, Ann.

MAX: But you and I can do anything together.

ANN: Cease! Max...I'm married. You can't fill in what's missing in my life any better than that stupid fantasy house could. Only I can do that. Even if you are Prince Charming, the maiden is right, there are no guarantees. No guarantees that I would be happy with you. No guarantees that I will be happy with Dave. Just faith. A lot of faith and a lot of work.

MAIDEN: A lot of work.

KING: And sacrifice. Don't forget sacrifice.

MAX: There's nothing I can say to change your mind?

ANN: No.

MAX: You gave me hope, you know? `Cause after Sharon died I just thought it was all over for me.

ANN: But it's not.

MAX: I don't know, Ann. I don't know.

ANN: You're a beautiful man. With a lot of love to give. It was a nice fantasy. With you, it was a very nice fantasy. But now we both have work to do. I have to keep building my marriage, and you have to start building your new house. (*She crosses to* DAVE).

(ERIC *enters.*)

DAVE: So you're coming back?

ANN: I was standing there, you know? Surrounded by a world of possibilities, and the phone was ringing. And I closed my eyes and tried to imagine perfection. I could have anything I wanted. Any whim immediately fulfilled in my mind's eye. I blinked and was surrounded by my perfect pottery. Blinked again and was surrounded by my perfect poetry. But in every imaginable permutation of perfection, I kept seeing you standing there with me. The two of us as kids filled with hope. That's all I've ever wanted.

DAVE: I love you.

ANN: I love you. And I'm sorry I left you like that. That was hurtful and irresponsible, but it was something I had to do.

DAVE: I know.

ANN: I want the world to be open for us. And I need you to hear me.

DAVE: You've opened my ears, believe me.

(*The* MESSENGER *enters.*)

MESSENGER: Alright. Mail's here. Got some messages to deliver. One for you.

(*The* MESSENGER *hands an envelope to* ANN, *which she opens.*)

DAVE: What is it?

(ANN *removes a hundred-dollar bill and reads the back of it.*)

ANN: "For the true winner." (*She tears it in two and hands half to* DAVE).

(DAVE *pops his half in his mouth and begins to chew.* ANN *does the same. They exit.*)

MESSENGER: One for you.

(MESSENGER *hands a letter to* MAIDEN, *which she looks at.*)

KING: What is it, my queen?

MAIDEN: It is from my father. We should visit him. I think he just might make a good grandfather.

(They exit.)

MESSENGER: And one for you. (*She gives* ERIC *a piece of pink stationery that has been taped together*)

(ERIC *looks at it for a beat. He smiles. He sits.*)

MAX: What does yours say?

MOE: It says have a cup of coffee and get on with your life.

(Blackout)

END OF PLAY